City Safari

Fox

Isabel Thomas

Heinemann
LIBRARY

Chicago, Illinois

To contact Capstone Global Library please phone 800-747-4992, or visit our web site www.capstonepub.com

Edited by Dan Nunn, Rebecca Rissman, and Helen Cox Cannons
Designed by Tim Bond
Original illustrations © Capstone Global Library Ltd 2014
Picture research by Mica Brancic
Production by Helen McCreath
Originated by Capstone Global Library Ltd
Printed and bound in China

17 16 15 14 13
10 9 8 7 6 5 4 3 2 1

Library of Congress Cataloging-in-Publication Data
Thomas, Isabel, 1980- author.
 Fox / Isabel Thomas.
  pages cm.—(City safari)
 Includes bibliographical references and index.
 ISBN 978-1-4329-8808-1 (hb)—ISBN 978-1-4329-8815-9 (pb) 1. Foxes—Juvenile literature. 2. Foxes—Behavior—Juvenile literature. 3. Urban animals—Juvenile literature. I. Title.

QL737.C22T485 2014
599.775—dc23   2013017408

Acknowledgments
The author and publisher are grateful to the following for permission to reproduce copyright material: Alamy p. 23 den (© blickwinkel/S Gerth); FLPA pp. 4 (Panda Photo), 10 (Roger Tidman), 13 (Phil McLean), 16 (Terry Whittaker), 20 (Jurgen & Christine Sohns), 23 earth (Jurgen & Christine Sohns), 23 scavenge (Panda Photo); Getty Images pp. 8 (Jim Dyson), 11 (Oli Scarff), 18 (David Strydom), 23 mate (David Strydom), 23 senses (Oli Scarff); Naturepl.com pp. 5 (Geslin/© Wild Wonders of Europe), 6 (© David Kjaer), 7 (2020VISION/© Terry Whittaker), 9 main (© Andy Rouse), 9 inset (© David Tipling), 12 (© Fabrice Cahez), 14 (© Laurent Geslin), 15 (Geslin/© Wild Wonders of Europe), 17 (2020VISION/© Bertie Gregory), 19 (Laurent Geslin), 21 (© Fabrice Cahez), 23 territory (Laurent Geslin); Shutterstock p. 23 roadkill (© Valeniker).

Front cover photograph of a fox reproduced with permission of Shutterstock (© Keith Livingston). Back photograph of a fox in a shed reproduced with permission of FLPA.

We would like to thank Michael Bright for his invaluable help in the preparation of this book.

Every effort has been made to contact copyright holders of any material reproduced in this book. Any omissions will be rectified in subsequent printings if notice is given to the publisher.

Warning!

Never touch wild animals or their homes. Some wild animals carry diseases. Scared animals may bite or scratch you. Never hold food for a fox to eat. It may bite your finger by mistake.

Note About Spotter Icon

Your eyes, ears, and nose can tell you if a fox is nearby. Look for these clues as you read the book, and find out more on page 22.

Contents

Who Has Been Caught Raiding the Trash Can? . . . 4

Why Do Foxes Live in Towns and Cities?. 6

What Makes Foxes Good at Living in
    Towns and Cities?. 8

Where Do Foxes Hide?. 10

What Do Foxes Eat?. 12

Why Do Foxes Like to Live Near People? 14

What Dangers Do Foxes Face in
    Towns and Cities? 16

Do Foxes Live Alone? 18

How Do Fox Cubs Learn to Live in
    Towns and Cities?. 20

Fox Spotter's Guide. 22

Picture Glossary. 23

Find Out More. 24

Index 24

Some words are shown in bold, **like this**.
You can find them in the glossary on page 23.

Who Has Been Caught Raiding the Trash Can?

Red-brown fur. Pointed ears. A bushy tail. It's a fox!

You don't need to go to the country to spot wild animals.

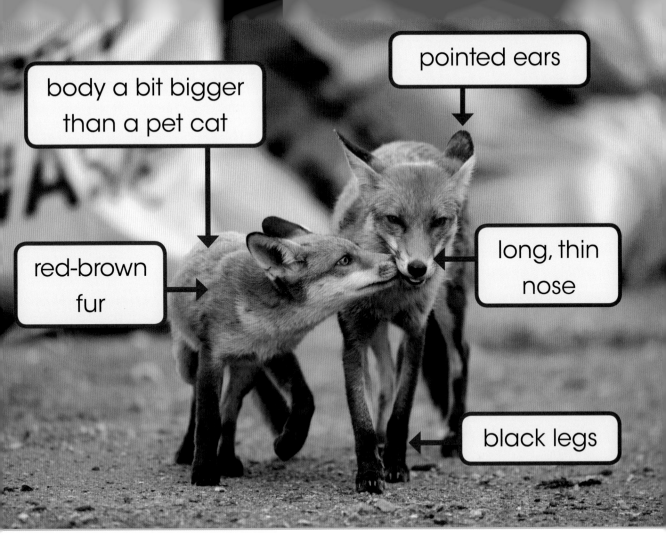

body a bit bigger than a pet cat

pointed ears

red-brown fur

long, thin nose

black legs

Thousands of foxes live in cities and towns.

Come on a city safari and find out if foxes are living near you.

Why Do Foxes Live in Towns and Cities?

Foxes live where they can find food, water, and shelter.

It's easy to find food where people live, and cities are warmer than the country.

You might spot foxes on golf courses, and in parks.

But their favorite city homes are big, messy backyards.

What Makes Foxes Good at Living in Towns and Cities?

Foxes can see, hear, and smell very well.

Their **senses** help them find food, even in the dark.

Foxes can run faster than a human sprinter and jump the height of a door.

These skills help them escape from danger quickly.

Where Do Foxes Hide?

Foxes make **dens** in hedges, compost piles, under sheds, and on roofs.

They like to hide from people during the day.

Look out for foxes just before dawn and just after dusk.

That is when they come out of their hiding places to find food.

What Do Foxes Eat?

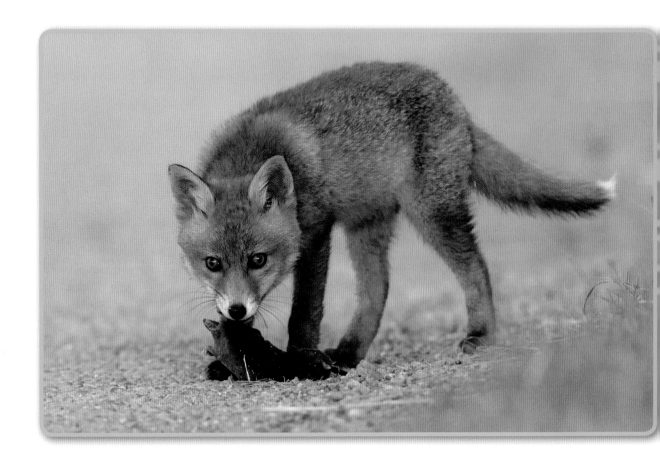

Foxes hunt small animals, such as rats, moles, birds, and insects.

They also eat food that they find, such as fruit and **roadkill**.

The area where a fox looks for food is called its **territory**.

Foxes leave signs such as droppings to warn other foxes to keep out!

Why Do Foxes Like to Live Near People?

Foxes sniff out food in trash cans, landfills, and on the streets.

Some people even put food out so that they can watch foxes in their backyards.

City foxes do not need to hunt as often as country foxes.

People throw away a lot of food, so foxes often find more than they can eat.

What Dangers Do Foxes Face in Towns and Cities?

hen house

Not everyone likes living near foxes.

Some people hunt or trap foxes to stop them from damaging backyards, or stealing pet chickens or ducks.

The biggest danger to city foxes is crossing the road.

Cars kill most city and town foxes before they are two years old.

Do Foxes Live Alone?

Foxes live in family groups, but they like to hunt and feed on their own.

Every winter, pairs of foxes get together to **mate**.

Foxes make lots of noise at that time of year.

Male foxes may fight to keep other males out of their **territory**.

How Do Fox Cubs Learn to Live in Towns and Cities?

Fox cubs are born in spring, in special **dens** called **earths**.

The whole family helps look after the cubs.

Fox cubs love to chase, play-fight, and chew everything they find.

Playing helps them learn how to hunt and **scavenge** for food.

Fox Spotter's Guide

1. Foxes have four toes on each foot. They leave diamond-shaped footprints with claw marks.

2. Foxes have special eyes that work well in the dark. This makes their eyes shine in bright light, such as car headlights. They may be the first thing you spot!

3. When foxes eat animals, their droppings are full of bone, fur, and feathers. They have a pointy twist at one end.

4. Foxes like to bury spare food to eat later. Look for signs of digging in flowerbeds and flowerpots.

5. Listen for fox calls, especially in winter. Male fox calls sound like three short barks. Female fox calls sound like screams.

Picture Glossary

 den hidden home of a wild animal

 earth special fox den where babies are born and looked after

 mate when a male and female animal get together to have babies

 roadkill dead animals that have been killed crossing roads

 scavenge look for food that has been thrown away or left over

 senses sight, hearing, smell, taste, and touch

 territory area that an animal lives in and defends from other animals

Find Out More

Books

Johnson, J. Angelique. *Red Foxes*. Mankato, Minn.: Capstone, 2011.

Leach, Michael. *Fox (Animal Neighbors)*. New York: Rosen, 2009.

Web sites

FactHound offers a safe, fun way to find Internet sites related to this book. All of the sites on FactHound have been researched by our staff.

Here's all you do:
Visit www.facthound.com
Type in this code: 9781432988081

Index

dangers 9, 16–17

dens 10, 20, 23

droppings 13, 22

earths 20, 23

food 6, 8, 11, 12, 14–15, 21, 22

footprints 22

fox cubs 20–21

mate 18, 23

scavenge 21, 23

senses 8, 23

territory 13, 19, 23